Goodbye, GASOLINE

The Science of **Fuel Cells**

by Kristi Lew

Content Adviser:
Jennifer Gangi, Program Director, Fuel Cells 2000

Science Adviser:
Terrence E. Young Jr., M.Ed., M.L.S.,
Jefferson Parish (Louisiana) Public School System

Reading Adviser:
Rosemary G. Palmer, Ph.D., Department of Literacy,
College of Education, Boise State University

Compass Point Books • 151 Good Counsel Drive, P. O. Box 669 • Mankato, MN 56002-0669

This book was manufactured with paper containing
at least 10 percent post-consumer waste.

Library of Congress Cataloging-in-Publication Data
Lew, Kristi.
  Goodbye, gasoline: the science of fuel cells / by Kristi Lew.
    p. cm. — (Headline Science)
  Includes index.
  ISBN 978-0-7565-3521-6 (library binding)
  ISBN 978-0-7565-3527-8 (paperback)
1. Fuel cells—Juvenile literature. I. Title. II. Series.
  TK2931.L49 2008
  621.31'2429—dc22   2008011729

Editor: Jennifer VanVoorst
Designers: Ellen Schofield and Ashlee Suker
Page Production: Ashlee Suker
Photo Researcher: Svetlana Zhurkin
Illustrator: Ashlee Suker

Art Director: LuAnn Ascheman-Adams
Creative Director: Keith Griffin
Editorial Director: Nick Healy
Managing Editor: Catherine Neitge

Photographs ©: Stuart Franklin/Getty Images, cover (bottom); Chiara Levi/iStockphoto, cover (inset, left), 25; Ben
Russell/iStockphoto, cover (inset, middle), 33; Scott Vickers/iStockphoto, cover (inset, right), 7; calvinng/iStock-
photo, 5; Jim Parkin/iStockphoto, 8; dgmata/iStockphoto, 9; Natalia Bratslavsky/iStockphoto, 10; imaginewithme/
iStockphoto, 11; Manfred Konrad/iStockphoto, 13; Friedrich Saurer/Alamy, 15; Wikimedia, public-domain image,
17 (left); Andi Berger/iStockphoto, 17 (right); Caro/Alamy, 19, 20; Ballard/IS/Visuals Unlimited, 21; Martin Bond/
Photo Researchers, 22; AP Photo/Douglas Healey, 26; Science Source/Photo Researchers, 27, 36; Julie Fisher/
iStockphoto, 28; José Luis Gutiérrez/iStockphoto, 29; Brad Mogen/Visuals Unlimited, 31; Toshifumi Kitamura/AFP/
Getty Images, 32; Robert Sullivan/AFP/Getty Images, 35; Don Wilkie/iStockphoto, 37 (left); Tor Lindqvist/iStock-
photo, 37 (right); Michael Klinec/Alamy, 39; Justin Sullivan/Getty Images, 40; Ben Blankenburg/iStockphoto, 41;
Scott Peterson/Liaison/Getty Images, 42; John James/Alamy, 43.

Visit Compass Point Books on the Internet at *www.compasspointbooks.com*
or e-mail your request to *custserv@compasspointbooks.com*

A BOOST FOR HYDROGEN FUEL CELL RESEARCH

>>> Lawrence Berkeley National Laboratory
January 25, 2007

The development of hydrogen fuel cells for vehicles [is] the ultimate green dream in transportation energy. ...

By converting chemical energy into electrical energy without combustion, fuel cells represent perhaps the most efficient and clean technology for generating electricity. This is especially true for fuel cells designed to directly run off hydrogen, which produce only water as a byproduct. ...

[According to scientist Vojislav Stamenkovic,] "Since the only byproduct ... is water vapor, their widespread use should have a tremendously beneficial impact on greenhouse gas emissions and global warming."

Imagine a future in which electricity can be produced without pollution. This clean energy can be used to power everything from cell phones to cars to office buildings. Even entire towns can be powered without polluting the environment. Many scientists and politicians believe such a future is possible. They believe that the future of global energy lies in devices called fuel cells. There are many types of fuel cells, but hydrogen provides the fuel for all of them.

AN ELECTROCHEMICAL DEVICE

Hydrogen fuel cells produce electricity by combining the elements hydrogen and oxygen. Inside the fuel cell, hydrogen and oxygen combine to make electricity. In the process of making electricity, the fuel cell also produces water. Because fuel cells change chemicals into electricity, they are called electrochemical devices.

Fuel cells are similar to another electrochemical device—the battery. Both store energy in a portable format. They make no noise while operating, and they have no moving parts to break down. The difference between a battery and a fuel cell is that a

Batteries are common electrochemical devices that share some characteristics with fuel cells.

KEEPING CURRENT

News changes every minute, and readers need access to the latest information to keep current. Here are a few key search terms to help you locate up-to-the-minute fuel cell technology headlines:

Advanced Energy Initiative of 2006

Energy Policy Act of 2005

fuel reforming

hydrogen economy

Hydrogen Fuel Initiative

proton exchange membrane (PEM) fuel cell

solid oxide fuel cell

zero emission vehicle

battery contains all of the chemicals it needs to make electricity. When these chemicals are used up by the battery, the battery "goes dead." A dead battery needs to either be thrown away or recharged. Fuel cells, on the other hand, require a constant flow of chemicals. These chemicals are supplied by fuel tanks. As long as fuel is flowing into the fuel cell, the fuel cell will continue to make electricity. So fuel cells do not really "go dead." They just need to be refilled, like the gas

tank in an automobile. However, you cannot pull up to a pump at your local gas station and fill up with hydrogen—at least, not yet.

AN ENERGY EMERGENCY

Scientists are working to make fuel cells a part of our energy reality. Currently about 70 percent of the electricity generated in the United States comes from the burning of fossil fuels such as coal, oil, and natural gas. Power plants burn coal

Hydrogen
Fuel

Someday hydrogen fueling stations may replace gas stations around the country.

school. But the United States can only produce about 40 percent of the oil consumed by Americans. The other 60 percent is purchased from other countries and imported.

There are other problems with fossil fuels as well. For one thing, fossil fuels are a nonrenewable source of energy. In other words, once these fuels are used up, they cannot be replaced in a short period of time.

The coal, oil, and natural gas being mined or pumped out of the ground today started out as plants and animals. These plants and animals lived about 290 million to 360 million years ago during the Carboniferous period. They died, decomposed, and eventually turned into fossil

to generate electricity to power our homes and businesses. Cars and buses burn gasoline to take us to work and fuels. Scientists are not sure exactly how these life forms turned into coal, oil, and natural gas, but they do know

Oil extraction is costly and sometimes environmentally damaging. There are many opportunites for oil to spill during its production, transportation, and consumption.

NOW YOU KNOW

The word *carboniferous* comes from the element carbon because all fossil fuels contain carbon. The Carboniferous period ended almost 40 million years before dinosaurs began to appear.

that it involved a lot of time, pressure, and heat. Over time, this heat and pressure caused the organisms to break down into simple hydrocarbons. These are organic molecules that are made up of the elements carbon and hydrogen.

The energy in fossil fuels is contained in the bonds between the hydrogen and carbon atoms. To get the energy out of the chemical bonds, the fossil fuels must be burned. When coal, oil, and natural gas burn, atomic bonds between the carbon atoms and the hydrogen atoms break, releasing energy in the form of heat and light. Energy is not the only thing that is released when fossil fuels are burned, however. Gases such as carbon dioxide, carbon monoxide, nitrogen oxide, sulfur dioxide, and methane are also released. These gases can be harmful to the environment.

GREENHOUSE GASES

Many scientists are specifically concerned about the amount of carbon dioxide that burning fossil fuels releases into Earth's atmosphere. They have found that the amount of carbon dioxide in the atmosphere today is at the highest level it has been for the last 650,000 years. This concerns the scientists because carbon dioxide is a greenhouse gas. Greenhouse gases allow heat from the sun to enter Earth's atmosphere, but they prevent the heat from escaping back out into space, too. This is called the greenhouse effect, because it is similar to the way a greenhouse traps heat to help the plants inside grow.

The greenhouse effect

Coal is created over millions of years as pressure and heat are naturally applied to decaying organic matter.

is necessary for Earth to support life. Without the greenhouse effect, the average global temperature would be about 0 degrees Fahrenheit (-18 degrees Celsius). However, trapping too much heat can make the planet heat up. This is called global warming. In 2007, scientists on the Intergovernmental Panel on Climate Control determined that global warming is "very likely" caused by human activities, such as burning fossil fuels. As a result, the scientists project that the average global temperature will likely rise. This increase in temperature could produce longer periods of unusually hot weather and stronger tropical storms. It could also cause

Human industry relies on the burning of fossil fuels, which releases harmful greenhouse gases into the atmosphere and contributes to global warming.

Global warming may be responsible for storms such as Hurricane Katrina, which devastated New Orleans, Louisiana, and other cities along the Gulf Coast in August 2005.

sea levels to rise.

Many scientists, environmental activists, and individual citizens believe that the harmful impact burning fossil fuels has on the planet is a good reason to find alternative sources of energy to run our cars, make electricity for our towns, and power our electronics. Hydrogen fuel contains three times more energy than gasoline and seven times more than coal. Because hydrogen fuel cells do not produce carbon dioxide or other greenhouse gases, they are considered a good source of alternative energy.

HYDROGEN FUEL CELLS POWER FUJITSU DATA CENTER

>>> CNet News
August 17, 2007

Hydrogen is a better source of energy than you think, according to Fujitsu.

The Japanese electronics giant inaugurated a 200-kilowatt hydrogen fuel cell from UTC (Power Company) on Friday that will provide electricity as well as heat to the buildings on its campus (in Sunnyvale, California).

The fuel cell—which sits in the parking lot and looks like a pair of giant green dumpsters—provides two types of energy to the facility. First, a unit heats methane with steam to create hydrogen. The hydrogen is passed through a proton exchange membrane (PEM). The electricity produced by the reaction with the PEM runs lights, computers and other equipment.

Hydrogen is the most abundant element in the universe. As much as 75 percent of the universe by mass is made up of hydrogen. It is very common in space, found in stars and giant gas planets such as Jupiter and Saturn. However, hydrogen gas is rare in Earth's atmosphere. Its light weight allows it to escape from Earth's gravity more easily than heavier gases. Still, hydrogen is the third most abundant element on Earth. But unlike in space, on Earth it is mixed with other things. For example, hydrogen can be found in chemical compounds such as water, alcohols, and hydrocarbons. It can also be found in plants and animals.

A BIT ABOUT ATOMS

To understand how a fuel cell uses hydrogen to create electricity, you need to know a bit about how atoms are put together. Atoms are the basic units of all matter. Matter is anything that has mass and takes up space. A desk, a chair, and a sandwich are all matter—and so is hydrogen. Atoms contain smaller units called subatomic particles. There are three main types of subatomic particles—protons, neutrons, and electrons. Protons have a positive charge and can be found in the nucleus, or the center, of the atom. Neutrons are also found in the nucleus, but they do not have a

The Horsehead Nebula is a swirling cloud of dust and gases; hydrogen gas creates the red glow behind the formation.

charge. They are neutral. The last type of subatomic particle, the electron, has a negative charge and is found outside the atom's nucleus. The attraction between the positively charged protons in the nucleus and the negatively charged electrons keeps the electrons moving around the out-side of the nucleus instead of floating off into space.

Hydrogen atoms have one proton, one electron, and no neutrons. They are always found bonded together as pairs in nature. Each hydrogen atom shares its single electron with another hydrogen atom so that two atoms share two electrons between them. Sharing electrons between two hydro-gen atoms bonds the atoms together and forms a hydrogen molecule.

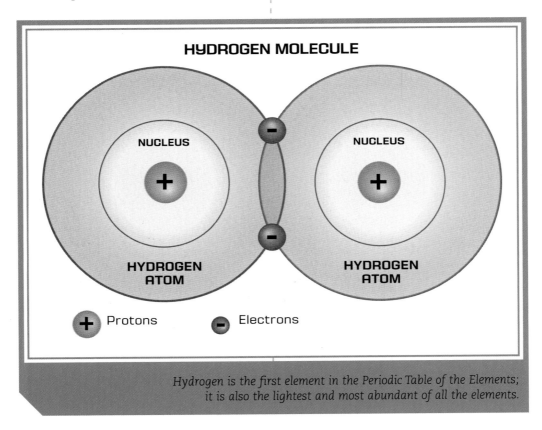

HYDROGEN MOLECULE

NUCLEUS + HYDROGEN ATOM

NUCLEUS + HYDROGEN ATOM

+ Protons   − Electrons

Hydrogen is the first element in the Periodic Table of the Elements; it is also the lightest and most abundant of all the elements.

HOW FUEL CELLS WORK

Electricity is nothing more than flowing electrons. That means that power can be generated by freeing electrons. Fuel cells rely on hydrogen for electrons. There are different kinds of fuel cells, each with different characteristics and uses. But every fuel cell has the same basic parts. They all have:

- A negative terminal, called an anode, and a positive terminal, called a cathode. A terminal is a point at which a substance can enter or exit a device.
- A catalyst, which is located next to each terminal. A catalyst is a special material that speeds up the reaction between hydrogen and oxygen.
- An electrolyte, which is located in the center of the fuel cell, between the catalysts. An electrolyte is a substance that can conduct an electric current when melted or dissolved in water. The electrolyte is the heart of the fuel cell. In a fuel cell, the electrolyte only allows protons to pass through it.

Fuel cells generate electricity in the following manner:

1. First, hydrogen is fed into the anode of the fuel cell. Oxygen from the air enters through the cathode. Channels in the anode and the cathode spread the gases evenly over the surface of the catalysts.

HEADLINE
SCIENCE

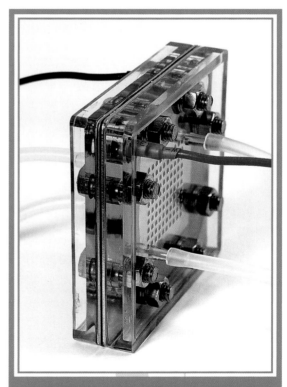

Hydrogen and oxygen enter the fuel cell through opposite sides.

2. The hydrogen molecules react with the catalyst. The reaction separates the protons and the electrons.

3. The protons pass through the electrolyte to the cathode.

4. The electrons cannot pass through the electrolyte and are forced to take a different path. As they travel, they create an electric current. The current powers one or more devices, such as motors or lights, that are included in the circuit.

5. After completing their circuit, the electrons join the protons at the cathode to form hydrogen molecules again.

6. Finally, because oxygen enters into the fuel cell at the cathode, the hydrogen combines with the oxygen to form

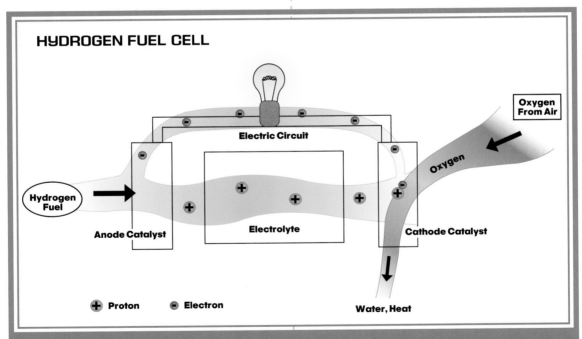

HYDROGEN FUEL CELL

Electric Circuit

Oxygen From Air

Oxygen

Hydrogen Fuel

Anode Catalyst

Electrolyte

Cathode Catalyst

➕ Proton   ➖ Electron

Water, Heat

Water and heat are the simple byproducts of the complicated chemical reaction that takes place inside a hydrogen fuel cell.

water. Water is made up of two hydrogen atoms and one oxygen atom.

The complicated chemical process that takes place inside a fuel cell results in two very uncomplicated byproducts: heat and water. An operating fuel cell produces clean energy with no pollution.

The water produced by a fuel cell is clean, pure water that is safe to drink.

THE FIRST FUEL CELL

Fuel cells are not a new idea. In fac the first fuel cell was made more than 150 years ago in 1839 by Sir William Robert Grove (1811–1896), a Scottish physicist. Grove knew tha sending an electric current throug water would split the water molecule into hydrogen and oxyger the two elements that make up water. So Grove decided to see what would happen if he reversed the reaction—combining hydrogen and oxygen to make electricity and water. Grove was successful and has come to be known as the father of the fuel cell. However, the term fuel cell was not used until 1889, when Ludwig Mond and Charles Langer used it to describe device that ran on air and coal gas

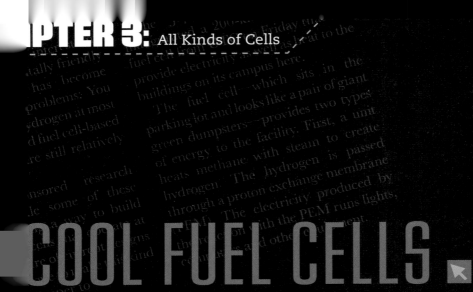

COOL FUEL CELLS

>>> NASA
March 18, 2003

Astronauts have been using [fuel cells] for power aboard spacecraft since the 1960s. Soon, perhaps, they'll be just as common on Earth—powering cars, trucks, laptop computers and cell phones.

In recent years the interest in bringing this environ-mentally friendly technology to market has become intense. But there are problems: You can't "fill 'er up" with hydrogen at most corner gas stations. And fuel-cell-based cars and computers are still relatively expensive.

By finding a way to build "solid oxide" fuel cells that operate at half the temperature of current designs ... [researchers] hope to make this kind of fuel cell both cheaper to manufacture and easier to fuel.

There are several types of fuel cells, each designed for different purposes. Although they produce electricity using the same process, they differ from one another in two ways. The most important difference is the electrolyte. Different electrolytes provide different voltages and different properties. Each type of fuel cell is generally named based on the electrolyte it uses.

PROTON EXCHANGE MEMBRANE (PEM) FUEL CELLS

The most practical fuel cell for use in cars, buses, homes, and businesses, according to the U.S. Department of Energy, is called a proton exchange membrane (PEM) fuel cell. In a PEM fuel cell, the electrolyte is a thin plastic membrane that looks like plastic wrap from your kitchen. One PEM fuel cell can make about

0.7 volts. Most car batteries are 12 volts. So to make the PEM fuel cell practical, many PEM fuel cells are combined to make what is called a fuel cell stack. Metal or carbon plates are used to connect the fuel cells so they can make enough power to run something useful, such as your family's car. Such a stack of PEM fuel cells is about the size of a microwave oven. Other fuel cells create a greater electrical output and so are much

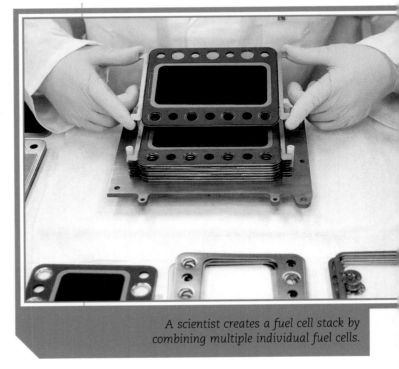

A scientist creates a fuel cell stack by combining multiple individual fuel cells.

larger. They range in size from a large central air conditioning unit to a compact car. These cells can provide greater amounts of electricity to power things such as an apartment complex, an office building, or multiple single-family homes.

Fuel cells also differ from one another based on their operating temperature. This is how hot the fuel cell needs to be in order to produce electricity. The PEM fuel cell is a good choice for transportation uses because its operating temperature is relatively low compared to other fuel cells. A PEM fuel cell runs at 140 to 176 F (60 to 80 C). As a result, the PEM fuel cell does not take a long time to warm up before it can make electricity. Other types of fuel cells must reach

The more fuel cells that are assembled in a stack, the more electricity the stack can generate.

temperatures as high as 1,832 F (1,000 C) before they will produce electricity. Because of their high operating temperature, these fuel cells are best suited for use as large, stationary power generators that produce electricity for towns or factories. This way, they do not have to be shut off and turned back on again. Their constant operation eliminates warm-up time.

PEM fuel cells are one of the more common types of fuel cells. But there are many other kinds of fuel cells that hold the same kind of clean energy promise. These include alkaline, phosphoric acid, molten carbonate, and solid oxide fuel cells.

A large stationary power generator contains many fuel cells stacked together to create a sizable electric output; the fuel cell stack is contained by a protective metal case.

OTHER TYPES OF FUEL CELLS

Alkaline fuel cells are one of the oldest fuel cells to be developed. The U.S. space program has used them since the 1960s. Alkaline fuel cells were used not only to create electrical power aboard the *Apollo* spacecraft, but also to create drinking water for the astronauts. This type of fuel cell is very expensive, however, so it is unlikely to be widely used outside of specialized applications.

The phosphoric acid fuel cell is the most commercially developed type of fuel cell. There are hundreds in use around the world. It uses phosphoric acid as its electrolyte. It has a higher operating temperature than a PEM fuel cell, so it requires a long warm-up time. This makes it unsuitable for use in cars. Instead, phosphoric acid fuel cells are used for larger-scale power generation. They are currently used in hospitals, hotels, nursing homes, and office buildings.

The PRODE power station in Milan, Italy, operates using phosphoric acid fuel cells, which are enclosed inside two large tanks.

Molten carbonate and solid oxide fuel cells are two other common types

FUEL CELL FAST FACTS

The five most common types of fuel cells differ from one another based on electrolyte, operating temperature, and uses.

Type of fuel cell	Electrolyte	Operating temperature	Uses
proton exchange membrane (PEM)	polymer membrane	140–176 F (60–80 C)	cars, portable power
phosphoric acid	phosphoric acid	212–428 F (100–220 C)	hospitals, office buildings
alkaline	alkaline potassium hydroxide	302–392 F (150–200 C)	U.S. space program, military vehicles
molten carbonate	molten alkaline carbonate	1,112–1,292 F (600–700 C)	power plants
solid oxide	hard ceramic metal	1,292–1,832 F (700–1,000 C)	power plants

Source: Fuel Cells 2000

of fuel cells. They are best suited for making power on a large scale, such as at a power plant. The high operating temperatures of these types of fuel cells provide a unique benefit. The high heat causes the water they produce to be released as steam. This steam can be used to run engines that in turn generate more power. The heat they produce can also be used to warm homes and businesses.

Though these fuel cells differ from one another in a number of ways, one thing they all have in common is fuel. Each needs a continuous flow of hydrogen in order to create power.

HIGH-TECH SIEVE SIFTS FOR HYDROGEN

National Science Foundation
February 2, 2006

Whether it's used in chemical laboratories or the fuel tanks of advanced automobiles, hydrogen is mostly produced from natural gas and other fossil fuels. However, to isolate the tiny hydrogen molecules, engineers must first remove impurities, and the currently available methods can require substantial equipment or toxic chemicals.

Now ... engineers have announced the development of a simpler, safer material that can potentially assist, and in some places replace, existing processing methods. The rubbery, plastic film, similar to membranes already in use in biomedical devices, has applications for isolating not only hydrogen, but also natural gas itself.

There are a few problems scientists must work out before fuel cells will be practical for everyday use. One of the hurdles that must be overcome is how to make fuel—that is, hydrogen—for the fuel cell.

ELECTROLYSIS

Although hydrogen is abundant in nature, it is usually part of a chemical compound such as water. To be used in a hydrogen fuel cell, hydrogen must be separated from other elements in a compound. Water can be split into its individual elements through a process called electrolysis. Electrolysis is the reverse of the reaction that occurs in a fuel cell. This process requires an electric current to be passed through the water. The electric current causes the water molecule to split into its parts—hydrogen and oxygen. The hydrogen can then be used as fuel.

Some scientists are experimenting

In electrolysis, an electric current separates the water molecule into hydrogen and oxygen so that the resulting hydrogen can be used in a fuel cell to create more electricity.

with fuel cells that are designed to run in reverse, or do electrolysis. The fuel cell would then be able to turn water back into hydrogen and oxygen when it is plugged into an electrical outlet at a home or business. This type of fuel cell is called a reversible fuel cell.

A car with a reversible fuel cell would be able to make some hydrogen from water stored onboard. To accomplish this, the car's electric motor would act as an electric generator, turning coasting or braking energy into electricity. The generated electricity, in turn, would be used by the reversible fuel cell to make hydrogen for later use.

FUEL REFORMING

Another way to produce pure hydrogen is through a process called fuel reforming. Fossil fuels such as natural gas, gasoline, diesel, and propane all contain large amounts of hydrogen

Fuel Cell Energy in Danbury, Connecticut, makes large stationary fuel cells that generate electricity for power plants while creating excess hydrogen that can be used as fuel.

that can be used as fuel for a fuel cell. Fuel reforming strips the hydrogen from the fossil fuel so that the hydrogen can be used to create power. For example, natural gas contains a hydrocarbon called methane. Methane is made up of one carbon atom and four hydrogen atoms. Natural gas can be transformed into pure hydrogen by a process called steam reforming. Steam reforming is the most common and least expensive method of producing hydrogen. In this process, methane is combined with steam at very high

Chemists at Argonne National Laboratory perform tests to assess the performance of TuffCell, a newly developed fuel cell.

temperatures—around 1,400 F (760 C). This reaction produces hydrogen, but it also produces carbon dioxide. So although the hydrogen it produces is a clean fuel, the process of creating it releases pollutants. Scientist Joseph Romm is critical of this method: "Using dirty energy to make clean energy doesn't solve the pollution problem—it just moves it around." And because fossil fuels are nonrenewable resources, fuel reforming is not a good long-term solution for producing hydrogen.

The United States currently produces about 10 million tons (9.07 million metric tons) of hydrogen per year, mostly with steam reforming of natural gas. This hydrogen is used for industrial purposes, such as making fertilizer and refining oil. If hydrogen-powered vehicles are to become the standard, the United States

GREEN GAS

One innovative way of making hydrogen fuel involves algae, simple plants that grow in water. Algae are a renewable resource that naturally create small amounts of hydrogen. Anastasio Melis, a scientist at the University of California at Berkeley, has found a way to make these organisms produce much more hydrogen than normal. As of 2008, the algae were not able to produce enough hydrogen to make the process cost effective. Someday, however, the process may be inexpensive enough to enable hydrogen to compete with coal or oil as a source of fuel.

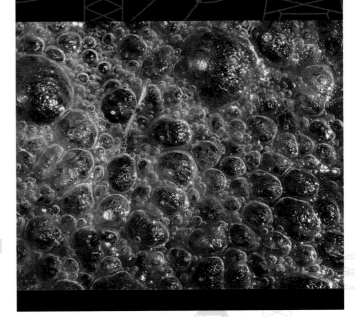

Wind farms, composed of multiple windmills, produce pollution-free power by capturing the energy of the wind and converting it to electricity.

will need to produce at least 10 times more.

In order for hydrogen fuel cells to help reduce greenhouse gases, such as carbon dioxide, scientists are focusing on ways to produce pure hydrogen using clean, renewable sources. These sources include wind, solar, and water power. For example, the power to produce hydrogen through electrolysis could come from wind power. Hydrogen could then be delivered by pipeline to a fueling station where people could get it. The entire process would avoid fossil fuels. This idea is broadly called the "hydrogen economy."

THE ZERO-ENERGY SOLUTION

>>> The New York Times
May 20, 2007

Mike Strizki's house, the house of the future, the revolutionary house that might very well change our lives forever, is an unremarkable two-story, 3,000-square-foot, white colonial-style kit home. ... There was nothing odd, or futuristic, or exotically "eco" about the house—no solar panels to be seen, no giant arrays of thermopane windows passively drinking up light and heat; yet here ... was a house that had the potential ... to help turn millions of American homes into fully self-sustaining power plants, each one capable of producing hydrogen to fuel cars as well.

A sign at the head of Strizki's long gravel driveway said, "Welcome to the first solar-hydrogen residence in North America."

Mike Strizki's solar-hydrogen house in suburban New Jersey is its own clean-energy power plant. It uses the energy collected by solar panels to generate the electricity to perform electrolysis. The electrolysis in turn produces hydrogen from water—hydrogen that is used to power fuel cells. These fuel cells can then create the electricity to run everything in the house, from lights to laptops. Houses like Strizki's may be one answer to making the hydrogen needed to fuel cars in the future. Scientists are working on solutions to other problems, too—problems such as how to make hydrogen in freezing temperatures, how to store hydrogen once it is made, how to get the hydrogen to the person who is going to use it, and how to make all of

More and more fuel cell hobbyists are beginning to build their own experimental fuel cells to provide additional clean, reliable power for their homes.

this cost about the same as gasoline does now.

FREEZING TEMPERATURES

The PEM fuel cell is the most promising type of fuel cell for most applications, but it has a unique complication. The electrolyte must contain water in order to allow protons to pass through the membrane. That is a problem for people who live in areas where temperatures fall below freezing. The proton exchange membrane will not work if it is frozen. Scientists are working to figure out how to keep the membrane moist in freezing temperatures.

STORING HYDROGEN

Once hydrogen fuel is produced, it must be stored. In order for fuel cell cars to compete with gasoline-powered ones, they must be able to carry enough hydrogen to go the same distance as a gasoline-powered car. That means that fuel cell cars must be able to travel about 300 miles (480 kilometers) before refueling. However, at temperatures above -423 F (-253 C),

Visitors to the 22nd World Gas Conference studied the power unit of Toyota's Fuel Cell Hybrid Vehicle (FCHV); Honda's FCX fuel cell vehicle is at the rear.

hydrogen is a gas. Gases take up more room than liquids, such as gasoline. So storing enough hydrogen in a car is a big problem. Currently two technologies seem to be the most promising—high-pressure compressed hydrogen gas tanks, and very-low-temperature liquid hydrogen tanks.

High-pressure compressed hydrogen gas tanks compress the hydrogen gas so it takes up less space. The hydrogen is under very high pressure—between 5,000 psi (pounds per square inch) and 10,000 psi. So these tanks must be very strong to prevent them from bursting. The compressed

HYDROGEN
FLAMMABLE GAS
NO SMOKING
NO OPEN FLAME

Hydrogen gas tanks require that hydrogen be stored under very high pressure.

hydrogen tanks in some hydrogen-fueled cars are reinforced with a material called carbon fiber. It is used because it is lightweight and strong. However, it is also very expensive.

Hydrogen is extremely flammable, so there are additional safety concerns involved in storing it. In its gaseous form, hydrogen is colorless, odorless, and tasteless. Artificial odors are added to other flammable, odorless gases to make sure a leak can be detected by smell. However, most fuel cells require very pure hydrogen. Adding an odor could damage or destroy the fuel cell. This makes detecting a leak very difficult. Researchers are working to develop sensors that can detect hydrogen leaks should the tank fail. Many studies, however, suggest that stored hydrogen is as safe, if not safer, than gasoline.

Hydrogen can also be stored as a liquid, but getting the hydrogen into liquid form requires temperatures below -423 F (-253 C). Liquid hydrogen tanks can store more hydrogen than compressed hydrogen gas tanks. However, a lot of energy is required to get the hydrogen cold enough to turn it into a liquid. Cooling the hydrogen uses about a third of the amount of energy that the hydrogen itself holds. These tanks are also very expensive.

NOW YOU KNOW

Hydrogen is sometimes burned as a fuel. It creates about three times as much energy as gasoline. The U.S. space shuttle and many other rockets burn liquid hydrogen mixed with oxygen.

COST

Storing hydrogen is not the only expensive part of a hydrogen fuel cell. The best catalyst for PEM fuel cells found so far is made of platinum, a precious and expensive metal. In addition to being expensive, platinum does not last very long as a catalyst. Byproducts of the reaction between

A liquid hydrogen tank vents in front of the space shuttle Discovery's boosters and fuel tank on the launch pad at Kennedy Space Center in Florida.

the platinum and the oxygen fuel cause the platinum to not work as well over time.

Scientists are experimenting with alloys of platinum to try to make a cheaper and more durable catalyst. An alloy is a mixture of two or more elements, at least one of which is a metal. Alloys generally have different properties from the individual elements of which they are made. In this case, scientists are hoping for a more durable platinum alloy that byproducts of the fuel cell reaction do not bind to as easily. Combining the platinum with other nonprecious metals such as nickel or cobalt may also decrease the cost.

HYDROGEN INFRASTRUCTURE

Another thing that will cost a lot of money is building a hydrogen infrastructure—the physical equipment needed for storage and delivery. For example, for the fossil fuels in use today, the infrastructure includes the following elements:

- Oil pipelines to move oil from the fields to the refining plants

A chemist at Brookhaven National Laboratory experiments with a material that holds promise as a new kind of catalyst for fuel cells.

The infrastructure for natural gas and oil delivery includes pipelines to move the fossil fuels from one place to another.

HELLO, HYDROGEN

Many countries are working hard to develop fuel cells as a source of clean, renewable energy. As of 2008, Iceland and Japan were leading the pack. But China is in a unique position to lead the world toward a global hydrogen economy. China is just beginning to develop a car culture. The nation recognizes that fossil fuels are a dead end. Chinese scientists believe fuel cells are the most promising technology for alternative energy. Because China doesn't have a well-developed gasoline infrastructure, it will be easier for the nation to establish a hydrogen economy. And with a population of more than 1.3 billion, whatever China does will have a big impact on the rest of the world.

- Refining plants that transform the oil pumped from the ground into forms that can be used in automobiles and other devices
- Gas stations that provide the fuel for customers

In order for cars powered by fuel cells to become a reality, an infrastructure for hydrogen fuel will need to be built. ◤

THE TRUTH ABOUT HYDROGEN

>>>>

Popular Mechanics
November 2006

When assessing the State of the Union in 2003, President Bush declared it was time to take a crucial step toward protecting our environment. He announced a $1.2 billion initiative to begin developing a national hydrogen infrastructure: a coast-to-coast network of facilities that would produce and distribute the hydrogen for powering hundreds of millions of fuel cell vehicles. Backed by a national commitment, he said, "Our scientists and engineers will overcome obstacles to taking these cars from laboratory to showroom, so that the first car driven by a child born today could be powered by hydrogen, and pollution-free."

The U.S. government has a goal to make fuel cell vehicles a practical, cost-effective alternative to fossil fuels by the year 2020. To help achieve this goal, President George W. Bush announced a program called the Hydrogen Fuel Initiative in his 2003 State of the Union address. This program, along with the Energy Policy Act of 2005 and the Advanced Energy Initiative of 2006, supports research in obtaining hydrogen, designing fuel cells, and making the equipment necessary to develop fuel cell technology and create an infrastructure. As of 2008, the U.S. government had dedicated more than $1.6 billion to fuel cell research and development.

HYDROGEN HIGHWAYS

The state of California has already started to build a hydrogen infrastruc-

A fuel-cell-powered bus took passengers for a ride in Berlin, Germany, at the 2006 Electric Vehicle Symposium.

ture. In 2004, California's governor, Arnold Schwarzenegger, signed an order to declare California's 21 highways "hydrogen highways." The order states that California will ensure that hydrogen-powered vehicles are available for consumers to buy by 2010. The state has also committed to building hydrogen fuel stations along its interstate highways. Since California residents buy one-fifth of all the cars sold in the United States, the example set by California will set the direction for the rest of the country.

Automotive manufacturers are working hard to make sure hydrogen-powered cars will be available. Currently all the major automotive manufacturers have a fuel cell vehicle either in development or in testing.

In 2004, California Governor Arnold Schwarzenegger signed an executive order to create the Hydrogen Highway Network.

In 2005, Honda leased the first commercial hydrogen car to a family in Redondo Beach, California. In 2008, Chevrolet put 100 fuel-cell-powered cars on the street for testing as part of its Project Driveway. As of spring 2008, General Motors and Toyota both had vehicles capable of driving more than 300 miles (480 km) without refueling. And Honda made its FXC Clarity fuel-cell-powered car available to customers in the summer of 2008.

POLITICAL IMPACT

As fuel cells become more widely used, their introduction will have social and political impacts. Today some countries are very rich because of the oil wells they own. Oil, which is turned into gasoline, is their most

SUGAR CELLS

Fuel cells that run on hydrogen are by far the most common type of fuel cell. But scientists are also working to develop fuel cells that use substances other than hydrogen to generate electricity. Researchers from St. Louis University are experimenting with a kind of fuel cell that runs on sugar. Enzymes, substances found in living cells, work as the catalyst. They break down the sugars to separate the electrons and produce an electrical current. Water is the only byproduct. Currently sugar-powered fuel cells are not capable of producing much power. But researchers believe that within a few years, these fuel cells may be able to power small electronic devices such as cell phones.

important export. It pays for their schools, roads, and government services. What will happen if cars stop using gasoline and instead run on hydrogen that can be made from water? Many countries have access to water, and they will no longer need to buy oil. The balance of power in the world is likely to change. The introduc-tion of a new technology—even one as potentially helpful as fuel cells—almost always upsets an existing way of doing things. This can also upset the social and political order and delay the use of a new technology as politicians and governments work through the issues.

الرازي

Saudi Arabia is the world's leading exporter of oil; more than 75 percent of the country's income comes from the sale of oil.

Chapter 6: *Our Fuel Cell Future*

A driver filled up a fuel cell vehicle at a hydrogen filling station at the University of Birmingham in England.

A HEALTHY FUTURE

With proper funding and continuing research, it is possible that the United States and other countries throughout the world will one day achieve hydrogen economies. People will drive zero- or near-zero-emission vehicles. It is hoped that reducing dependence on fossil fuels will help to reduce pollution and improve Earth's air and water qualities. This, in turn, will improve our health. Because electric vehicles powered by fuel cells can help reduce the amount of greenhouse gases being released into the atmosphere, they may reduce the possibility of further global warming. Using fuel cells to power our cars, homes, and electronic equipment may one day pave the way to a cleaner, healthier future for us all.

HEADLINE SCIENCE

43

1839
Sir William Robert Grove makes the first fuel cell; he calls his invention the "gas voltaic battery"

1889
Ludwig Mond and Charles Langer coin the term *fuel cell*

1932
Francis Bacon builds the first practical fuel cell

1959
Harry Karl Ihrig demonstrates the first fuel-cell-powered vehicle: a tractor

1960s
General Electric develops a fuel cell for NASA's *Gemini* and *Apollo* spacecrafts

1986
Ballard Power Systems develops the first PEM fuel cell that produces enough power to make running a car off of a fuel cell a possibility

1993
The world's first hydrogen filling station opens in California; Ballard Power Systems develops and demonstrates the first hydrogen fuel-cell-powered bus

1997
Daimler Benz and Toyota launch prototype fuel-cell-powered electric cars

1998
Canada's first hydrogen fueling station opens; Ford gets a prototype fuel cell engine

2002
The U.S. Department of Energy (DOE) and the United States Council for Automotive Research announce a partnership to advance research for affordable hydrogen fuel cell vehicles

2003
President George W. Bush announces the $1.2 billion Hydrogen Fuel Initiative in his State of the Union address

2004
Ford's Fuel Cell Vehicle Program is launched

2005
The Energy Policy Act of 2005 offers consumers and businesses tax credits for buying hybrid-electric cars and installing fuel cell power plants in buildings they own

2006
DOE offers $100 million for research projects that will help solve the problems of hydrogen fuel cells

2008
Chevrolet puts 100 fuel-cell-powered cars on the street for testing; Honda offers its FXC Clarity fuel-cell-powered car for sale in the summer

Timeline

GLOSSARY

alloy
mixture of two or more elements, at least one of which is a metal

anode
negative terminal of a fuel cell where electrons are stripped from the hydrogen atom

atom
basic building block of all matter

catalyst
substance that speeds up a chemical reaction without being used up by the chemical reaction

cathode
positive terminal of a fuel cell where oxygen, hydrogen ions, and electrons combine to make water

electricity
flow of electrons

electrolysis
process of using an electric current to cause a chemical change

electrolyte
substance that is capable of conducting an electric current when melted or dissolved in water

electron
negatively charged subatomic particle found outside the nucleus of an atom

element
substance that cannot be broken down into a smaller substance; primary component of matter

fossil fuel
coal, oil, and natural gas that originated from ancient organisms

fuel cell
device that creates elecricity through a chemical reaction between hydrogen and oxygen

hydrocarbon
chemical compound made up mainly of hydrogen and carbon atoms

molecule
small bit of matter made of two or more atoms bonded together

proton
positively charged subatomic particle found in the nucleus of an atom

proton exchange membrane (PEM) fuel cell
type of fuel cell that uses a thin plastic membrane as its electrolyte; most practical fuel cell for use in cars, buses, homes, and businesses

terminal
point through which a substance can enter or exit a device

volt
unit for measuring the force of an electrical current or the stored power of a battery

FURTHER RESOURCES

ON THE WEB

For more information on this topic, use FactHound.

1. Go to *www.facthound.com*
2. Type in this book ID: 0756535212
3. Click on the *Fetch It* button.

FactHound will find the best Web sites for you.

FURTHER READING

Hayhurst, Chris. *Hydrogen Power: New Ways of Turning Fuel Cells Into Energy*. New York: Rosen Publishing Group, 2003.

Miller, Kimberly. *What If We Run Out of Fossil Fuels?* New York: Children's Press, 2002.

Morgan, Sally. *From Windmills to Hydrogen Fuel Cells: Discovering Alternative Energy*. Chicago: Heinemann Library, 2007.

Solway, Andrew. *Hydrogen Fuel*. Milwaukee: Gareth Stevens Pub., 2007.

LOOK FOR OTHER BOOKS IN THIS SERIES:

Climate Crisis: The Science of Global Warming

Cure Quest: The Science of Stem Cell Research

Great Shakes: The Science of Earthquakes

Nature Interrupted: The Science of Environmental Chain Reactions

Rise of the Thinking Machines: The Science of Robots

SOURCE NOTES

Chapter 1: "A Boost for Hydrogen Fuel Cell Research." Lawrence Berkeley National Laboratory. 25 Jan. 2007. 22 April 2008. www.lbl.gov/Science-Articles/Archive/MSD-H-fuel-cells.html

Chapter 2: Michael Kanellos. "Hydrogen Fuel Cells Power Fujitsu Data Center." CNet News. 17 August 2007. 22 April 2008. www.news.com/Hydrogen-fuel-cells-power-Fujitsu-data-center/2100-11392_3-6203247.html?tag=topicIndex

Chapter 3: "Cool Fuel Cells." NASA. 18 March 2003. 22 April 2008. http://science.nasa.gov/headlines/y2003/18mar_fuelcell.htm

Chapter 4: "High-Tech Sieve Sifts for Hydrogen." National Science Foundation. 2 Feb. 2006. 22 April 2008. www.nsf.gov/news/news_summ.jsp?cntn_id=105797

Chapter 5: Mark Svenvold. "The Zero-Energy Solution." *The New York Times*. 20 May 2007. 22 April 2008. www.nytimes.com/2007/05/20/magazine/20solar-t.html?_r=1&oref=slogin

Chapter 6: Jeff Wise. "The Truth About Hydrogen." *Popular Mechanics*. November 2006. 22 April 2008. www.popularmechanics.com/technology/industry/4199381.html

ABOUT THE AUTHOR

Kristi Lew is the author of more than 20 science books for teachers and young people. Fascinated with science from a young age, she studied biochemistry and genetics in college. After graduation, she worked in genetic laboratories for more than 10 years and taught high school science. When she's not writing, she enjoys sailing with her husband, Simon, aboard their small sailboat, *Proton*. She lives, writes, and sails in St. Petersburg, Florida.

INDEX